LAURA K. MURRAY

grow with me

KOALA

CREATIVE EDUCATION · CREATIVE PAPERBACKS

Published by Creative Education
and Creative Paperbacks
P.O. Box 227, Mankato, Minnesota 56002
Creative Education and Creative Paperbacks are
imprints of The Creative Company
www.thecreativecompany.us

Design by Ellen Huber
Production by Travis Green
Art direction by Rita Marshall
Printed in Malaysia

Photographs by Alamy (blickwinkel, imageBROKER,
Steve Taylor ARPS), Corbis (Corbis, Suzi Eszterhas,
Suzi Eszterhas/Minden Pictures, D. Parer & E. Parer-
Cook, Gerry Pearce, Joel Sartore, Carol Sharp),
Getty Images (James Hager, Cameron Spencer),
iStockphoto (Kitch Bain, benjamint444, Craig Dingle),
Newscom (Suzi Eszterhas), Shutterstock (BMCL, Liv
Falvey, Eric Isselee, Ekaterina Kamenetsky, Marcella
Miriello, zhaoyan), SuperStock (NHPA/NHPA)

Library of Congress Cataloging-in-Publication Data
Murray, Laura K.
Koala / Laura K. Murray.
p. cm. — (Grow with me)
Includes bibliographical references and index.
Summary: An exploration of the life cycle and life
span of koalas, using up-close photographs and step-
by-step text to follow a koala's growth process from
embryo to joey to mature koala.

ISBN 978-1-60818-562-7 (hardcover)
ISBN 978-1-62832-163-0 (pbk)
1. Koala—Infancy—Juvenile literature. 2. Koala—Life
cycles—Juvenile literature. I. Title.
QL737.M384M874 2015
599.2'5—dc23   2014028006

CCSS: RI.3.1, 2, 3, 4, 5, 6, 7, 8; RI.4.1, 2, 3, 4, 5, 7; RF.3 3, 4

First Edition HC 9 8 7 6 5 4 3 2 1
First Edition PBK 9 8 7 6 5 4 3 2 1

TABLE OF CONTENTS

Koalas are **mammals** called marsupials (*mar-SOOP-ee-ulz*). A marsupial spends time in its mother's **pouch** after it is born. Some people call koalas "koala bears," but the animals are not bears.

Koalas are found in the forests of eastern Australia. They live in **eucalyptus** (*yoo-kuh-LIP-tus*) trees. Koalas eat the leaves and branches. They sleep for 18 to 20 hours each day!

4

A koala sleeps in different positions to warm up or cool down.

5

6 *Koalas like to sit in the forks and nooks of tall trees for hours.*

Koala fur can be gray or brown. A koala has white fur on its chest, arms, and ears. It has a large nose, too. Koalas have clawed paws and curved bodies that are good for climbing trees. Koalas do not have full tails, but their padded bottoms help them sit on branches.

Koalas weigh 9 to 30 pounds (4.1–13.6 kg). Koalas that live in southeastern forests are bigger than koalas to the north. The southern koalas grow thicker fur, too.

7

The fur of southern koalas may be darker and browner.

A mother koala gives birth to a baby koala. When the baby koala is born, it is only 0.8 inches (2 cm) long. That is the size of a jelly bean!

The baby is called a joey. It does not have hair or ears yet. As soon as the joey is born, it knows just what to do. The joey uses its senses of smell and touch to crawl into its mother's pouch. The pouch opens near the mother's back legs.

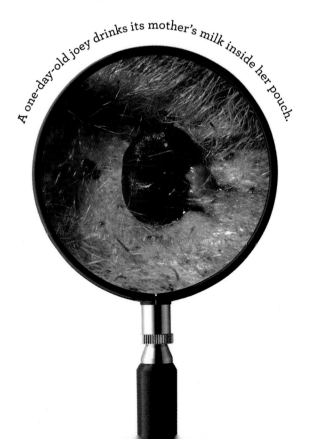

A one-day-old joey drinks its mother's milk inside her pouch.

The joey develops eyes, ears, and fur as it grows inside the pouch.

9

10 *Mothers and joeys enjoy a close bond during the first year.*

A joey stays safe in its mother's pouch for many months. It drinks its mother's milk. At 22 weeks old, the joey has a light coat of fur. It opens its eyes. Within the next eight weeks, the joey gets its first teeth and full coat. It eats **pap** that its mother's body makes from the food she eats.

A joey comes out of the pouch when it is six to seven months old. It still nurses from its mother and rides on her back. The joey tries out climbing and eating leaves, too.

11

By the time a koala is one year old, it is too big to fit inside a pouch. It stops drinking its mother's milk. The koala must feed itself. It uses its paws to grip branches and put leaves in its mouth.

Koalas have five **digits** on their paws. Each front paw has two thumbs. The young koala finds eucalyptus leaves for meals. Sometimes koalas eat other kinds of leaves or plant parts, but they are very picky eaters!

12

A koala uses its extra thumbs to better grip tree branches.

Koalas eat only a few
dozen of the 700-some
kinds of eucalyptus.

13

Eucalyptus leaves can be crushed into oil for making cough drops.

14 A grown koala eats one to two pounds (0.5–0.9 kg) of leaves each day. Eucalyptus leaves are **poisonous** to most animals. But the pap that joeys eat gets their bodies ready to **digest** (*die-JEST*) eucalyptus.

A koala hardly ever drinks water. It gets all the moisture it needs from plants. Eucalyptus does not give koalas much energy. That is why koalas move slowly and sleep so much.

Koalas tend to be most active at night, sleeping in the daytime.

15

16 *Koalas whose home ranges overlap may share certain trees.*

When it is one to three years old, a koala leaves its mother. Adult koalas live by themselves in areas called **home ranges**. The young koala must find a home range of its own.

A koala uses several trees in its home range for food and shelter. Sometimes a koala jumps from tree to tree. A male koala rubs his chest on tree trunks to mark the territory with his scent.

17

A koala leaps among tree branches only if the distance is short.

A koala may share a home range with an-other koala. Females often share a home range that is controlled by an **alpha** male. Other males may make their homes in the area, too.

But koalas do not like company. They sleep and eat alone. They visit other koalas only when it is mating season.

18

A mature male can be identified by the long brown mark on his chest.

Koalas may meet while keeping cool near the forest floor.

19

20 *A male koala's low bellows sound like human snoring or burping.*

Koalas are ready to mate when they are two or three years old. Around this time, they reach their full length of two to three feet (61–91 cm). Mating season lasts from August to February.

A male mates with the females in his home range. He lets out deep, loud sounds called bellows to attract a mate. Koalas also scream or snort to show fear or annoyance. Mother koalas may hum or click at their children.

21

After koalas mate, the male does not help raise the joey.

A joey begins as an **embryo** (*EM-bree-oh*) inside its mother's **womb**. The embryo grows inside the mother koala for 34 to 36 days. Then the joey is born. It continues growing inside its mother's pouch.

A female koala gives birth every one to three years. The koala stays with its mother until a new joey is born. Then it leaves home.

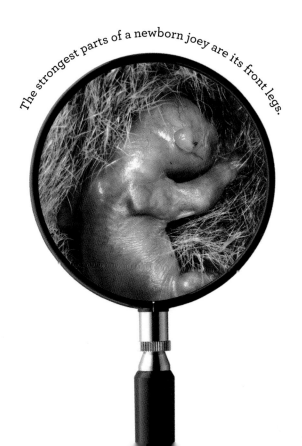

The strongest parts of a newborn joey are its front legs.

Older female koalas usually do not give birth every year.

23

24 *Australia's wildfire season lasts from September to February.*

Dingoes and other dogs with tall ears have the best hearing.

Koalas like to be safe in the trees. If a koala is on the ground, it can be attacked. **Predators** such as dogs, birds, or dingoes (wild dogs) eat koalas. Other koalas get sick and die.

Koalas need many trees to survive. Wildfires or **drought** destroy the forests that koalas use for food and shelter.

25

Years ago, the first people to live in Australia sometimes hunted koalas for food. Starting in the late 1800s, Europeans killed millions of koalas for their fur. People used the **pelts** to make coats and rugs.

Today, it is against the law to hunt koalas. Many people try to protect these animals. But humans destroy koala **habitat**. They cut down eucalyptus forests to build roads or homes.

Rescue workers try to keep koalas safe from cars and people.

Some koalas live in special areas that are protected by laws.

Koala teeth wear down over the years, making eating difficult.

28 Koalas can live 13 to 17 years in the wild. Koalas that live near people and busy roads might die much sooner. A koala may die, but its young will live on. Later, new joeys will be born. They will grow up and climb among the tall eucalyptus trees.

A mother koala carries her joey as she climbs, eats, and sleeps.

An embryo grows inside a mother koala for 34 to 36 days.

A joey is born and crawls  into its mother's pouch.

The joey drinks milk and develops teeth and fur.

At 22 weeks old, the joey begins feeding on its mother's pap.

After 6 to 7 months, the joey comes out of the pouch.

At 1 year old, the young koala eats only leaves.

Between the ages of 1 and 3, a koala finds a home range.

A koala is ready to mate when it is 2 to 3 years old.

After 13 to 17 years, a koala dies.

alpha: *most powerful*

digest: *to turn food into another form*

digits: *fingers or toes*

drought: *a time with little rain*

embryo: *a baby in its early stages of development before birth*

eucalyptus: *a type of Australian evergreen tree whose leaves produce oil*

habitat: *the home of an animal*

home ranges: *areas in which animals live and travel*

mammals: *animals that usually grow hair or fur and give birth to live young*

pap: *a soft and runny form of droppings made from a mother koala's diet of eucalyptus*

pelts: *skins of an animal with the fur still on*

poisonous: *causing death or illness*

pouch: *a fold of skin with one opening*

predators: *animals that kill and eat other animals*

womb: *the place where babies develop before they are born*

31

WEBSITES

Ranger Rick: Koala Kid
http://www.nwf.org/Kids/Ranger-Rick/Animals/Mammals/Koalas.aspx
Learn more about koalas and play animal games.

San Diego Zoo: Koala Cam
http://zoo.sandiegozoo.org/cams/koala-cam
See what koalas are doing right now at the San Diego Zoo!

Note: Every effort has been made to ensure that the websites listed above are suitable for children, that they have educational value, and that they contain no inappropriate material. However, because of the nature of the Internet, it is impossible to guarantee that these sites will remain active indefinitely or that their contents will not be altered.

READ MORE

Bodden, Valerie. *Koalas*.
Mankato, Minn.: Creative Education, 2009.

Owen, Ruth. *Koalas*.
New York: Windmill Books, 2014.

32

INDEX